PSYCHE & EROS

THE LADY AND THE MONSTER

A
GREEK
MYTH

GRAPHIC UNIVERSE™

STORY BY
MARIE CROALL

PENCILS AND INKS BY
RON RANDALL

EUROPE

*A*DRIATIC
*S*EA

G
R
E
E
C
E

▲
MOUNT
OLYMPUS

*A*EGEAN
*S*EA

*M*EDITERRANEAN
*S*EA

PSYCHE & EROS

THE LADY AND THE MONSTER

B LACK
S EA

A
GREEK
MYTH

A S I A

M I N O R

ORACLE
AT DIDYMA

GRAPHIC UNIVERSE™ MINNEAPOLIS ● NEW YORK

In Greek mythology, Mount Olympus is home to the most important gods and goddesses. These deities rule over nature and over all aspects of human life—such as love, marriage, death, and the afterlife. The ancient Greek people honored the gods and goddesses with prayer and gifts. In return, the deities interacted with human individuals, sometimes to the person's benefit and sometimes to his or her great misfortune.

Psyche is a mortal woman who gets drawn into the world of gods and goddesses. Her great beauty attracts both good and bad attention on Mount Olympus. She draws the jealous anger of Aphrodite, the goddess of love. At the same time, Psyche wins the love of Aphrodite's son, Eros, the god of passion. As many Greek myths do, Psyche's story weaves together human nature and divine power.

STORY BY MARIE CROALL

PENCILS AND INKS BY RON RANDALL

COLORING BY HI-FI DESIGN

LETTERING BY MARSHALL DILLON AND
TERRI DELGADO

CONSULTANT: THERESA KRIER, PH.D.,
MACALESTER COLLEGE

Graphic Universe™
A division of Lerner Publishing Group, Inc.
241 First Avenue North
Minneapolis, MN 55401 U.S.A.

Website address: www.lernerbooks.com

Library of Congress Cataloging-in-Publication Data

Croall, Marie P.
    Psyche & Eros : the lady and the monster : a Greek myth / story by Marie Croall ; pencils and inks by Ron Randall.
       p.   cm. — (Graphic myths and legends)
    Includes index.
    ISBN-13: 978-0-8225-7177-3 (lib. bdg. : alk. paper)
    1. Psyche (Greek deity)—Juvenile literature.
    2. Eros (Greek deity)—Juvenile literature.
    3. Aphrodite (Greek deity)—Juvenile literature.
    I. Randall, Ron. II. Title.
    BL820.P8C76 2009
    741.5'973—dc22   2007043353

Manufactured in the United States of America
1 2 3 4 5 6 - DP - 14 13 12 11 10 09

TABLE OF CONTENTS

A BEAUTIFUL MAIDEN ... 6

AN ANGRY GODDESS ... 10

A SORROWFUL WEDDING ... 13

A MYSTERIOUS HUSBAND ... 18

A PAIR OF JEALOUS SISTERS ... 23

A PARADISE LOST ... 28

IMPOSSIBLE TASKS ... 33

GLOSSARY AND PRONUNCIATION GUIDE ... 46

FURTHER READING ... 47

CREATING *PSYCHE & EROS* ... 47

INDEX ... 48

ABOUT THE AUTHOR AND THE ARTIST ... 48

A BEAUTIFUL MAIDEN

THERE ONCE WAS A PROSPEROUS GREEK CITY.

THE CITY WAS RULED BY A WISE AND NOBLE MAN.

HE WAS A FAIR RULER. BUT MORE THAN HIS LAWS AND HIS CITY, HE WAS KNOWN FOR HIS DAUGHTERS.

THE ELDEST DAUGHTERS WERE PRETTY AND CHARMING.

BUT THE YOUNGEST, PSYCHE, WAS MORE BEAUTIFUL THAN ANY WOMAN WHO HAD EVER LIVED.

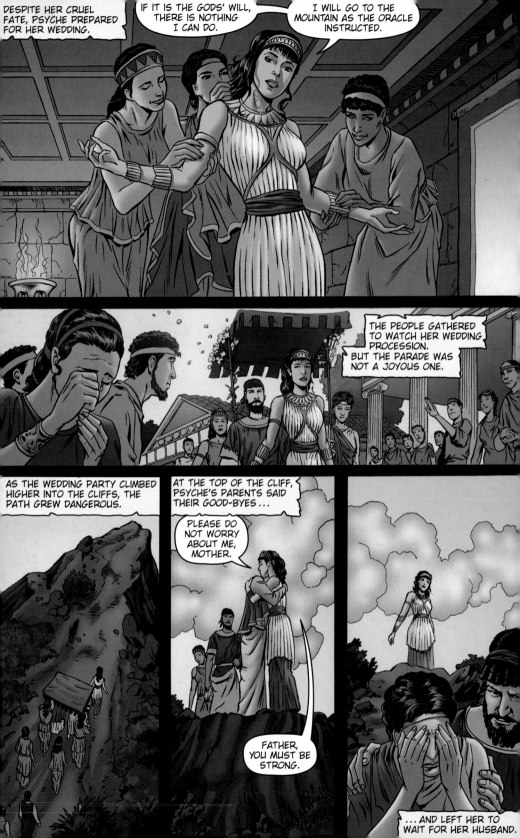

PSYCHE WAITED FOR A LONG TIME.

AND THEN...

...SOMEONE CAME FOR HER.

19

A PARADISE LOST

PSYCHE WAITED IN VAIN FOR HER HUSBAND TO RETURN.

SHE STOPPED SLEEPING AND EATING.

ALL SHE THOUGHT OF WAS HER BELOVED EROS.

AT LAST, PSYCHE DECIDED THAT IF SHE WANTED HER HUSBAND BACK, SHE WOULD HAVE TO FIND HIM.

SHE SET OFF IN SEARCH OF HIM.

SHE SEARCHED IN TEMPLES IN THE CITIES.

SHE SEARCHED IN TEMPLES BY THE OCEANS.

BUT SHE FOUND NOTHING.

PSYCHE TURNED NEXT TO HERA, THE GODDESS OF MARRIAGE.

HERA, YOU ARE THE PROTECTOR OF ALL MARRIED WOMEN.

PLEASE HELP ME FIND MY HUSBAND.

CHILD, THIS IS NOTHING I CAN HELP YOU WITH.

I HAVE NO TIME FOR APHRODITE'S JEALOUSY.

THERE'S NO AID FOR ME HERE.

I KNOW WHAT I MUST DO NOW.

30

SYCHE MADE HER WAY TO
HE ISLAND OF CYPRUS.

THERE SHE KNEW SHE WOULD
FIND A BITTER ENEMY...

...BUT ALSO THE ONLY
ONE WHO COULD HELP HER.

APHRODITE?

YOU'VE COME
TO BEG FOR
MY HELP?

YOU ARE
THE ONLY ONE
WHO CAN TAKE
ME TO MY
HUSBAND.

THAT'S
RIGHT.

I
CAN.

BUT WHY
SHOULD I?

WHAT ARE YOU DOING HERE? YOU DON'T BELONG HERE!

HROUGH THE CAVERN, PSYCHE EACHED THE RIVER STYX, THE OUNDARY OF THE UNDERWORLD.

BUT THE FERRYMAN, CHARON, REFUSED TO TAKE HER ACROSS THE RIVER.

PLEASE, I MUST SPEAK WITH HADES.

CHARON WAS CHARMED BY PSYCHE'S BEAUTY. HE AGREED TO FERRY HER ACROSS THE STYX.

SOMETHING HAS GUIDED ME HERE. IF THE GODS WISH ME TO SEE HADES, YOU DON'T WANT TO INTERFERE, DO YOU?

BUT ON THE OTHER SHORE, PSYCHE FACED A FIERCER OBSTACLE— THE GUARDIAN OF THE GATES TO THE UNDERWORLD ...

BUT CERBERUS, TOO, WAS CHARMED BY PSYCHE AND LET HER PASS THROUGH THE GATES UNHARMED.

. CERBERUS, THE HREE-HEADED DOG.

SNNNRRRRL!

RAAARRRRR!

GRRRRR

... ARRR ...

GLOSSARY AND PRONUNCIATION GUIDE

APHRODITE (*a*-fro-*dye*-tee): the Greek goddess of love

CERBERUS (*sehr*-buh-ruhs): a fierce, three-headed dog that guards the entrance to the underworld

CHARON (*kair*-on): the boatman who guides souls across the river Styx into the underworld

CYPRUS (*sy*-pruhs): an island in the Mediterranean Sea near Turkey. Cyprus was traditionally thought to be the home of Aphrodite.

DEMETER (*dim*-eh-tur): the Greek goddess of the harvest and of agriculture

EROS (*ehr*-ahs): Aphrodite's son and the Greek god of passion

HADES (*hay*-dees): the Greek god of the underworld

HERA (*hehr*-uh): the Greek goddess of marriage and childbirth, married to Zeus

MOUNT OLYMPUS (uh-*lim*-puhs): a mountain in northeastern Greece. The ancient Greeks believed the mountain was home to the gods and goddesses, who each had a palace there.

NAIAD (*nay*-uhd): in Greek myth, a type of female spirit who lives in rivers, streams, springs, and other bodies of fresh running water

ORACLE (*or*-uh-kuhl): speech in which a god reveals a hidden truth or foretells a future event, or the place where that happens. The ancient Greeks believed that the gods spoke through special priestesses who lived in temples or in isolated places, such as caves.

PERSEPHONE (per-*sef*-uh-nee): Demeter's daughter and Hades's wife

PSYCHE (*sy*-kee): a beautiful princess who falls in love with Eros

STYX (stiks): the river that encircles the underworld. Once the souls of the dead were ferried across the Styx by Charon, they could not return to the world above.

UNDERWORLD: the kingdom of the dead, ruled over by Hades. In Greek mythology, the souls of the dead traveled to the underworld, where Hades decided their eternal fate. Living mortals were not allowed in the underworld.

ZEPHYRUS (*zeh*-fuh-ruhs): the Greek god of the west wind

ZEUS (zoos): the main Greek god, the ruler of Mount Olympus

FURTHER READING

Bolton, Lesley. *The Everything Classical Mythology Book: Greek and Roman Gods, Goddesses, Heroes, and Monsters from Ares to Zeus.* Avon, MA: Adams Media Corporation, 2002. This who's who guide introduces young readers to Greek and Roman mythology.

Day, Nancy. *Your Travel Guide to Ancient Greece.* Minneapolis: Runestone Press, 2001. Day prepares readers for a trip back to classical Greece, including which cities to visit, how to get around, what to wear, and how to fit in with the locals.

Hamilton, Edith. *Mythology.* Boston: Little, Brown & Co., 1942. Hamilton's classic book focuses on the stories of Greek gods and heroes, but it also covers Roman and Norse myths.

Macdonald, Fiona. *Gods and Goddesses in the Daily Life of the Ancient Greeks.* New York: Peter Bedrick Books, 2001. Macdonald provides an introduction to the traditions and religious beliefs of the ancient Greeks. Using photographs, illustrations, and detailed diagrams, the book looks at how these beliefs affected daily routines, entertainment and literature, and events such as birth and death.

CREATING *PSYCHE & EROS*

In retelling Psyche's tale, Marie Croall drew upon classical and modern sources including *The Story of Eros and Psyche* by Apuleius, translated by Edward Carpenter. Artist Ron Randall used books on ancient Greek history, clothing, and architecture and photographs of Greek art to shape the story's visual details. And consultant Theresa Krier provided expert guidance on historical details, textual accuracy, and classical pronunciation.

original pencil sketch from page 6

INDEX

Aphrodite, 8, 9, 29, 30, 31, 32, 43; gives impossible tasks to Psyche, 33–41; sends Eros to wound Psyche, 10–11

Cerberus, 42
Charon, 42, 43
Cyprus, 31

Demeter, 29

Eros, 10, 22, 23, 26–27, 32; falls in love with Psyche, 11–13; hides his identity from Psyche, 20–21; rescues Psyche, 44–45

Hades, 29, 41, 42, 43
Hera, 30

Mount Olympus, 29

naiad, 38–39

oracle, 13, 14–15

Persephone, 29, 43
Psyche: draws Aphrodite's anger, 9–10; goes to the mountain to be married, 16–17; listens to her sisters' advice, 25; meets her new husband, 20–21; performs Aphrodite's impossible tasks, 33–41; reunited with Eros, 45; searches for Eros, 28; sneaks in to see Eros, 26–27

underworld, 41, 42–43

Zephyrus, 18, 19, 24
Zeus, 44–45

ABOUT THE AUTHOR AND THE ARTIST

MARIE P. CROALL lives in Cary, North Carolina, with her husband and four cats. She has written for Marvel, DC Comics, Moonstone Books, Devil's Due, and Harris Comics. Her other Graphic Myths and Legends work includes *Ali Baba: Fooling the Forty Thieves*, *Marwe: Into the Land of the Dead*, and *Sinbad: Sailing into Peril*. She has also completed a self-published graphic novel and a short film. She has spent much of her life reading fables and legends and enjoys discovering new things about different cultures.

RON RANDALL has drawn comics for every major comic publisher in the United States, including Marvel, DC, Image, and Dark Horse. His Graphic Myths and Legends work includes *Thor & Loki: In the Land of Giants*, *Amaterasu: Return of the Sun*, *Beowulf: Monster Slayer*, and *Tristan & Isolde: The Warrior and the Princess*. He has also worked on superhero comics such as *Justice League* and *Spiderman*; science fiction titles such as *Star Wars* and *Star Trek*; fantasy adventure titles such as *DragonLance* and *Warlord*; suspense and horror titles including *Swamp Thing*, *Predator*, and *Venom*; and his own creation, *Trekker*. He lives in Portland, Oregon.